LET IT GO

A Journal for Releasing the Bad
& Embracing the Good

Christine Schultz

CASTLE POINT BOOKS

www.castlepointbooks.com

The Castle Point Books trademark is owned by Castle Point Publishing, LLC.
Castle Point books are published and distributed by St. Martin's Publishing Group.

ISBN 978-1-250-27642-1 (trade paperback)

Design by Tara Long
Images used under license by Shutterstock.com

Our books may be purchased in bulk for promotional, educational, or business use.
Please contact your local bookseller or the Macmillan Corporate and
Premium Sales Department at 1-800-221-7945, extension 5442, or by email at
MacmillanSpecialMarkets@macmillan.com.

First Edition: 2021

10 9 8 7 6 5 4 3 2 1

This Journal belongs to:

You can't experience simple joys when you're living life with your hair on fire.

EMILY LEY

INtroDuctiON

WELCOME TO THE SWEET TREAT OF SERENITY! This little gift of mindful ambrosia can be yours through the practice of learning to let go of all that's holding you back. As you journey toward that reward, walk confidently around the drama that doesn't belong to you, take care of what does, and let go of the idea that you can fix everything. Is that a dumpster fire ahead? Sounds like a job for a professional, so take care of yourself instead and don't get burned. When you let go of unrealistic expectations, constant comparisons, wearisome grudges, and everything else weighing you down, you'll discover a smoother road toward a sweeter, lighter place. This journal is your guide to getting there.

Every page of *Let It Go* features fun paths to finding release and cruising freely to happy moments and meaningful goals. Whether you travel the pages in order or hop around the scenic stops, creative prompts help you clearly see roadblocks in your life and blast through to better views and the place you really want to be—where sunshine, peace, and possibilities surround you.

So get ready to loosen your grip on old routes and baggage, go off-road as needed, and steer toward new refreshing destinations!

Swing Your Way Free

When you're still holding on for dear life to what once meant so much to you (a job title, a place, another person's praise), your hands may cramp and your arms start to feel like gelatin. That's your signal that it's time to release your grip and reach forward. Fill in the rung where you feel stuck right now, the handholds that can launch you, and that wild dream of a destination.

READY TO MOVE
FROM HERE:

FINALLY,
FREE!

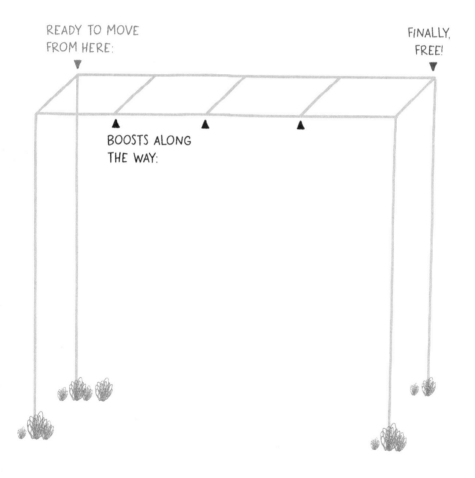

BOOSTS ALONG
THE WAY:

Like the monkey bars, you have to let go to move forward.

LEAH BUSQUE

A bend in the road is not the end of the road... unless you fail to make the turn.

HELEN KELLER

Hang on for the Ride

Whether taking a road trip or just cruising through your day, not knowing where you're going can be scary. But it can also lead to the most blockbuster experiences along the way. What change, big or small, is coming down the pike that you don't feel ready to navigate? Add it to the road map below.

What scenic overlook could you discover down that rutted road that would make your trip worth taking? Add it on the signpost above.

Welcome That Change

We often resist change with every ounce of our being, but it can sometimes be just what we need. What item of clothing helps you let go of your outside world and worries and relax into a more creative state of mind? Maybe it's a chef's hat, an artist's smock, or simply a pair of fuzzy bunny slippers. Attach a photo of yourself wearing the item or draw it below.

Life is like underwear: change is good.

UNKNOWN

The question isn't who is going to let me; it's who is going to stop me.

UNKNOWN

Take a Chance on You

You don't need a permission slip from anyone but yourself! In the form below, write the words that give you authority to do whatever you've been wanting to do in your life—no matter how big or small, crazy or sane in others' eyes. Wave your permission slip in the mirror and go be the powerhouse that you are.

PERMISSION SLIP

FOR:

TO:

Embrace the Mess

We often long for only the pretty picture of life, but it can be both beautiful and messy at the same time. Grab a marker in your favorite color and scribble in the space below. Go ahead, make a mess! Enjoy the crazy jumble of your spirited self.

What does it feel like to let loose without expectations centered on a certain (admit it, perfect) outcome? Is there an area of life where you need to release perfection in favor of forward motion?

The thing that
is really hard,
and really amazing,
is giving up on
being perfect and
beginning the work
of becoming
yourself.

ANNA QUINDLEN

When you reach
for the stars,
you may not
quite get one,
but you won't
come up with a
handful of mud,
either.

LEO BURNETT

See a Clear Sky

Whether you're longing to explore a remote location or launch a new career, what wild idea would you go after if there was nothing stopping you?

Imagine any perceived blocks fading into the darkness, then circle or write in the words that best describe what motivates you.

RECOGNITION

CONTRIBUTION

CREATIVITY

PEACE OF MIND

CURIOSITY

ADVENTURE

CONNECTION

KNOWLEDGE

Make time tonight (or some night soon) to look up at the stars and envision grabbing hold of your sparkly dream.

Turn Up the Volume

What songs make you pulse? Create your playlist for good vibes, energy, and inspiration below. Then whenever you need some release, hit Play. But don't just listen. Belt out the words. Drum or strum in the air. Dance, dance, dance! No one's watching—for real, or tell yourself that.

If you hit a wall, climb over it, crawl under it, or dance on top of it.

UNKNOWN

The pessimist
complains about
the wind;
the optimist
expects it to change;
the realist adjusts
the sails.

WILLIAM ARTHUR WARD

Decide to Sail

Of course, we'd love the wind to direct our sails toward that beautiful coastal paradise with the golden sunsets and little umbrella drinks, but sadly, we can't magically make it blow our way. Rather than sink the boat, let's learn to sail.

What three things do you complain about on a weekly basis that are beyond your control?

1   2   3

What three things do you keep hoping will magically go away?

1   2   3

If your friend kept clinging to unrealistic expectations, what would you tell them to do?

With that advice in mind, how can you shift your own attitudes or actions to put the wind in your sails?

Call Out the Spam

Imagine you could hit the Unsubscribe button for your coworkers' rants, your neighbors' nosy intrusions, and your relatives' unwanted criticisms. In the "inbox" below, note the daily irritations that get dumped on you. Next to the ones that you can truly classify as "not my problem," check Unsubscribe and in clear words report why you're leaving the fuss behind.

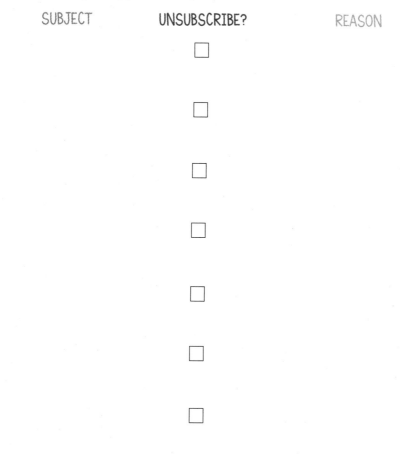

SUBJECT   UNSUBSCRIBE?   REASON

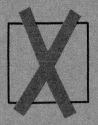

PLEASE cancel my subscription to your issues.

UNKNOWN

For now,
it's just you,
the world,
and the
sunrise.

UNKNOWN

Turn Off the Anxiety Alarm

Mornings can make or break your mood for the rest of the day. So don't just slide out of bed on autopilot! Plan ways to let go of any anxiety and fuel yourself with positive energy instead. What wake-up song or alarm sound will get you moving with a smile?

From fresh flowers to a favorite photo, what feel-good items will you place on your bedside table so they are the first things you see in the morning?

What message can you post for yourself on your bathroom mirror or coffee maker that will inspire you for the rest of the day?

GO DOWN the Wrong Road

It happens all the time: as soon as we turn in the wrong direction, we suddenly know which way we should've gone. So try this to get out of your own head: Think about a yes/no choice you're facing—should you _____

_____?

First, imagine you've decided yes. Set off in that direction on the road below. Draw or write what happens and how you feel if you go that way.

Now pretend you've gone the opposite way. Describe above what happens when you say no.

Which way would you rather go?

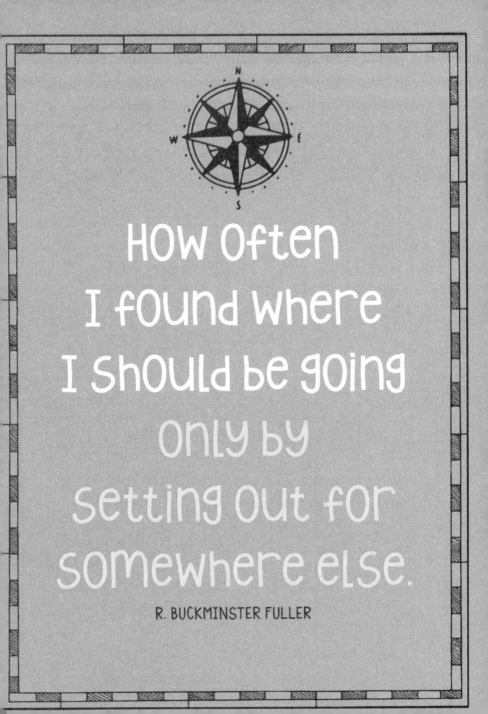

HOW Often
I found where
I should be going
Only by
Setting out for
Somewhere else.

R. BUCKMINSTER FULLER

NOt forgiving
is like drinking
rat POison and
then waiting for
the rat to die.
ANNE LAMOTT

Escape the Rat Trap

What grudge have you been holding on to that has your shoulders or stomach in a knot? Acknowledge it for what it is by putting it in the waste bin below. Then draw a skull and crossbones over it or write "Danger: Toxic" in bold lettering over the top. Envision hazmat experts hauling it off while you find something more fun to fixate on.

Find Your Thrill

When the big kids did it, it looked like pure fun, but then your turn came. What scared the bejeezus out of you as a kid that you so wanted to do? Did you do it anyway? How did it feel?

What gives you that thrill now that you're grown, and when is the next chance you can feel alive in that experience?

Life is like
a roller coaster.
You can either
scream every time
there is a bump or
you can throw
your hands up and
enjoy the ride.

UNKNOWN

Other people's lives
seem better than
yours because
you're comparing their
director's cuts
with your behind
the scenes.

EVAN RAUCH

Roll Out the Red Carpet

Grab some popcorn and sit back for the show. If a movie were made of your life, what obstacles would the hero be challenged to overcome?

What events that seemed to last forever in real time are only a quick passing scene in the overall picture?

What would be the happiest ending?

Wish You Were Here

If you could pack your bags and run away, where would you go? Paris? Patagonia? The Met? Even though you probably can't jet off right now, make a list of steps you can take to move toward your destination (learn to speak French or Spanish, research travel spots, tour the museum online, etc.). Star the one step you'll take this week.

Of the gladdest
moments in
human life...
is the departure
upon a distant
journey into
unknown lands.

SIR RICHARD BURTON

The universe buries strange jewels deep within us all, and then stands back to see if we can find them.

ELIZABETH GILBERT

Discover Your Gems

Time to explore all the tunnels in your life to find the treasures in you! What do your friends and family love most about you? (Not sure? Ask!) What do you secretly (or not-so-secretly) believe you're good at? Write your gifts on the jewels below, then let them shine as you go about your days.

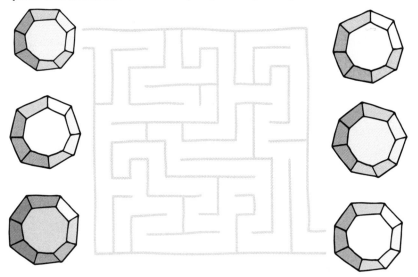

In what areas are you clearly not gifted? List areas you can release so others can shine. We can't do it all!

Drop the Overthinking

Are you hesitating to dig into that sundae topped with sprinkles and whipped cream? Do you get cold feet as you step to the edge of the diving board? Does your second, third, or fourth-guessing keep you from the good stuff? In what areas of your life do you need to say *enough already!* and just jump into the enjoyment?

Life is
short,
so make
it sweet.

UNKNOWN

Noise is an imposition on sanity, and we live in very noisy times.

JOAN BAEZ

create some Quiet

Enough with the drama already! The same petty situations day after day make you want to pull your hair out. What are these people even saying? Grab a pencil and write the craziest ramblings you've heard this week in the speech bubbles below.

Now take a big eraser and wipe out the noise to go from *blah, blah, blah* to *ahhh!*

YOU GOt ThiS!

It's going to be okay. Really. There is no need to run a marathon or climb Mount Everest in troubled times when we really just need to drink some tea, sit in the bath, and be kind to ourselves.

What hardships are you sitting with now?

What would you say to a friend who is sitting with the same hardships?

Say those words to yourself.

You don't need
to get an "A" in
surviving
a pandemic.
Making it through
is good enough.

NATALY KOGAN

A spring wind
blew my list
of things
to do away.

GREG BROWN

Free Your Day

Pretend you're a kid on Saturday morning with the whole day free. Check off the things that are your favorite kind of fun, or write your own in the space provided. Then make a playdate with yourself and go have a blast.

☐ BUILD A FORT.

☐ READ A GOOD BOOK.

☐ RIDE YOUR BIKE.

☐ HIKE INTO THE WOODS WITH YOUR FRIENDS.

☐ LIE IN A FIELD AND WATCH THE CLOUDS.

☐ GO FISHING.

☐

☐

☐

☐

☐

☐

☐

☐

Share Important Words

Fear can keep us from sharing all sorts of feelings. What words are you holding back that could make a difference in a relationship? Write them here, then set a time and place to say the words face-to-face.

You might not be out to fight dragons today, but bravery isn't all about swords & charging into battle.

JANE SCEARCE

I have been known on occasion to howl at the moon.

CRASH DAVIS

Let Out the Goof

We all feel a need to do outlandish things from time to time—and that's completely normal. What urges to howl at the moon have you given into lately?

How did it feel to let a little bit (or a lot!) of oddness out?

What's up next on your get-impulsive list?

Ready, Set, Stop?

You've finally topped the hill and are ready to coast happily into the sunset, but for some reason you're stomping on the brake. Wait?! What? Check off the reasons you hold yourself back from happiness, big or small.

☐ I DON'T DESERVE TO FEEL THE WIND IN MY HAIR.

☐ I'M NOT GOOD ENOUGH.

☐ SOMEONE ELSE DESERVES IT MORE THAN ME.

☐ I'M SCARED OF SUCCESS.

☐ _____

[Insert your own ridiculous reason here.]

Now cross those negative thoughts out and—with your brightest marker—write why you deserve to feel the joy.

Use fear
as an engine,
not a brake.

PAULO COELHO

YOU are not
required to set
yourself on fire
to keep other
people warm.

UNKNOWN

UP in Smoke

If you're a parent, a caretaker, or simply a kind soul, your peace of mind probably flames up on a daily basis. Well, it's time to warm your own heart for a change. Make yourself a cup of cocoa, put on your fluffy robe, grab your favorite pens, and draw a bonfire circle. Inside, write or sketch the things you'd like to set on fire to save your sanity.

Choose Your Snack Pack

We all need little pick-me-ups to get us through the day. What are the guilty pleasures (celebrity mags, coffee, true crime TV, chocolate, wine...) that comfort you?

What are your healthy healers (hugs, walks, books, the gym, houseplants...)?

If you had enough energy bars to power you to wherever you wanted to go, where would it be?

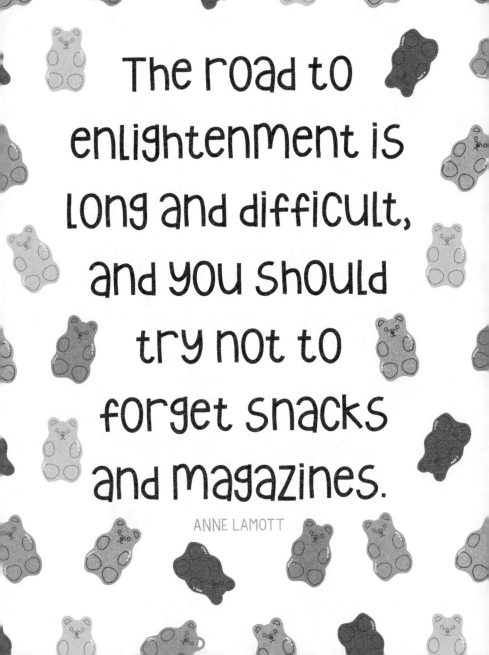

The road to enlightenment is long and difficult, and you should try not to forget snacks and magazines.

ANNE LAMOTT

MONSTERS
are real,
and ghosts
are real too.
They live
inside us...

STEPHEN KING

Dance with Your Monster

Ding dong the witch is dead, but other things still scare us—rejection, growing old, looking dumb, not measuring up. Imagine your fear as the monster beneath your bed. Describe or draw what the creature looks like.

Now invite your monster out to play. Draw yourself riding on its shoulders, romping through the jungle, or lying down beside it for a nap. You might not make that beast your bestie, but seeing it as a little less scary will do you nicely.

YOU BE YOU

Those random freckles, that raucous laugh, the hitch in their walk—we love those quirky traits in our rock stars and rom-com heroes, but not so much in ourselves. Well, why the heck not? It is time to embrace what makes you *you*. Own it! What unique characteristics do your fans love most about fabulous you?

Embrace what makes you unique, even if it makes others uncomfortable.

JANELLE MONÁE

Give me a lever long enough and a fulcrum on which to place it, and I shall move the world.

ARCHIMEDES

Catapult Your Way to Success

There's got to be a better way to get this dang boulder over the hill. What seemingly impossible goal are you trying to accomplish? Write it on the boulder below.

Now let go of the idea that you have to complete this feat alone! Think of the people or apps or organizations that could help you lift the weight. Write them on the lever below. How amazing would it feel to launch that load sky-high?!

Happy Mountain Day!

There's a fabulous tradition at many colleges called "Mountain Day"—the college president chooses a beautiful fall day to call off classes and set the students free to climb a mountain or picnic in the park. We all need a tradition like that, whether it's beach days or snow days or family fun days. Describe or draw one of your favorite memories from playing hooky below.

Now, pull out the calendar and add an upcoming designated day for fun and freedom.

The
mountains
are calling
and I
must go.

JOHN MUIR

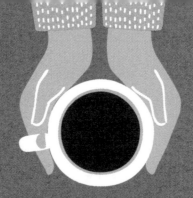

GOOd COMPANY
in a journey
Makes the way
seem shorter.

IZAAK WALTON

Gather Your Team

If you were traveling into the wilderness, who would be on your survival team, and what would they contribute to keep everyone sane and alive? Don't forget to note what you would contribute!

TRAVELER	CONTRIBUTION

Who is in your life now that would be better for you to leave behind in order to make progress on your journey? Is there other baggage it would be wise to leave behind?

Don't Just Chase Your Tail

Time to take your creativity out to play. Where does it lead? Check off your favorite new trick to try, or make up one of your own in the space provided, then let your creative collie off its leash.

- [ ] OPEN A COOKBOOK TO A RANDOM PAGE—
NOW GO MAKE THE RECIPE!

- [ ] HEAD TO THE BEACH AND COLLECT SHELLS,
STONES, BEACH GLASS, OR DRIFTWOOD TO USE
IN YOUR HOME DECOR.

- [ ] PICK A PROJECT FROM ONE OF THOSE PINTEREST
BOARDS AND ACTUALLY DO IT!

- [ ] LEARN CALLIGRAPHY AND WRITE A LETTER
TO AN OLD FRIEND.

- [ ] PICK UP KNITTING, CROCHETING, OR NEEDLEPOINTING,
AND FIND A FRIEND TO JOIN IN OR A CHARITY
FOR DONATIONS.

- [ ]

- [ ]

- [ ]

Possessing a
creative mind, after all,
is something like
having a border collie
for a pet:
it needs to work
or else it will cause
you an outrageous
amount of trouble.

ELIZABETH GILBERT

YOU were
my cup of tea,

but I drink

champagne now.

UNKNOWN

Fill Your Cup

Enough with the lame excuses and lousy treatment! Time to choose friends who love you for you. What have you let a friend or love interest get away with? Write a toast calling them out.

What sparkly emotions do you feel when you find friends who nourish you? Write a toast celebrating what they mean to you.

Naughty and Nice

We're not all one thing or the other. Some days we stick to the speed limit (or at least we're close), fold the laundry, and know how to filter our opinions. Other days we feel the wind in our hair, go skinny-dipping, and let every thought flow out our mouths without pause. Embrace both sides of you below. On the left, list your gold-star behaviors. On the right, list your wild-side traits.

SOME days,
I want to be
PRIM and PROPER,
and others,
I want to be
in a band.

MELISSA MCCARTHY

Boredom is the feeling that everything is a waste of time;
serenity, that nothing is.

THOMAS SZASZ

StOP, LOOk, LiSten

We interrupt your regularly scheduled busy-being-busy programming to bring you a moment of zen. You've probably heard that gratitude lights up the regions in your brain that fill your body with well-being and serenity, right? So let's pause for a moment of gratitude. What small moments of wonder give you joy? They could be as simple as listening to the birds sing outside or watching a beloved person or pet sleep.

Make it a habit each day to soak in these moments of sweet serenity.

Connect the Dots

It's hard to let go of the idea that one accomplishment leads perfectly to the next and pushes you up the ladder to success. But—*newsflash!*—life doesn't happen in a straight upward line, even when we're going from Point A to Point B. Connect the dots below, then write in some actions you've taken that you thought would steer you in one direction but that actually led you in another that had its own unforeseen rewards.

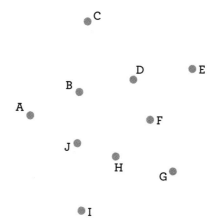

What interesting things came out of what seemed like a long detour (or even wrong turn) at the time?

Straight lines go too quickly to appreciate the pleasures of the journey.

RENÉ CREVEL

If you want
an interesting
party sometime,
combine cocktails
and a fresh box
of crayons.

ROBERT FULGHUM

Let's Party!

Who said the kids get to have all the fun? Go raid the craft closet. Get out the crayons, the markers, the paints. Pour yourself your favorite drink and use the space below to splash some random acts of color. This is the fun part. This is you!

Day and Night

Ever feel like you're trying to make something (or someone) into something it's not? Once you've sunk a lot of time and effort in, it's hard to let go. To get a clue whether you're clinging too tightly, check the boxes that apply to you in either of the two columns below.

TRYING HARD

☐ Doing it for the joy of it

☐ Seeing things for what they are

☐ Enjoying the creative journey

☐ Being happy with whatever happens

☐ Being free to move on

TRYING TOO HARD

☐ Doing it for a certain result only

☐ Wanting it to be something it's not

☐ Being overstressed and watchful

☐ Tying your self-worth to the finish line

☐ Holding on no matter what

Is there an area in your life on which you need to release your grip?

A day without sunshine is like,

you know,
night.

STEVE MARTIN

There is a superhero in all of us. We just need the courage to put on the cape.

SUPERMAN

It's a Bird, It's a Plane!

If you could jump into the nearest phone booth—assuming they still existed—and change into your cape and tights, what would your superpower be? Draw or describe it here.

How would you use your superpower for good?

What costume (or power pose) do you use to help you feel more mighty?

Say What?

Of course, we all want to be liked. So when someone says something harsh, it's easy to obsess. But negative feedback from negative people says more about them than you. In the space below, write the hurtful comments you have received over the years. Then release the words' hold on you by scribbling over them. (And if you need constructive feedback, stick to the people you trust!)

Whatever
People think
Of Me is
none Of
MY business.

RUPAUL

This life is mine alone. So I have stopped asking people for directions to places they've never been.

GLENNON DOYLE

Map Your Own Path

So many opinions—some of them invited, some not! What answer do you keep looking to other people for when you know deep down that only *you* hold the answer that's right for you?

How can you focus to hear your own inner voice more clearly over all the clamor that surrounds you?

Be Your Own Boss

When we were kids, the adults controlled our choices, but now that we're grown-ups (sort of), it's time to take charge of our own daily diets. In the columns below, write what you want more or less of in your life.

YES, PLEASE!   NO THANKS!

AS a Child my
family's menu
consisted of
two choices:
take it or leave it.

BUDDY HACKETT

TOO much of
a good thing
can be
wonderful.

MAE WEST

Let It Overflow

Sure, some things are better in moderation. But have you ever had a day when you laughed too much? Loved too much? Had too much time to play with pets and hang out with your favorite humans? List the people, places, and activities that always fill you with joy.

How can you find ways to take in more of that good life?

Use Envy to Energize

When you feel envy rising, you have a choice: wallow in resentment or rewire your envy toward inspiration. Whom do you envy and what do you envy about that person—their confidence, relationships, career, money?

Now, get more specific about what you see that inspires you. For example, their confidence allows them to meet lots of people, or money enables them to travel.

What's one step you could take to follow in their direction? Could you take a public speaking course or start a travel savings account? Those brown shoes can go far!

Did you ever
get the feeling
that the world
was a tuxedo
and you were
a pair of
brown shoes?

GEORGE GOBEL

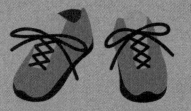

It's easier to
go down a hill
than up it,
but the view
is much better
at the top.

HENRY WARD BEECHER

Reach the TOP

What hard things—from morning runs and cleaning your car to visiting with difficult relatives and making a case for a raise—do you find worth doing once you've gotten to the top?

What uphill climb are you putting off right now that would lead to a magnificent view? Who or what could help you get your feet moving?

Ditch the Daily Grind

It's easy to get swept along by whatever comes our way. Then we look up and say, "Wait! Where did the last year just go?" Habits can help us take hold of each day with intention. What ten things do you spend most of your time doing daily?

1.

2.

3.

4.

5.

6.

7.

8.

9.

10.

Mark a star next to the choices that are getting you where you want to go. Are there any choices left without stars? Ask yourself if you can cross out at least one and replace it with something more in tune with what you want to be doing.

HOW we spend our days is, of course, how we spend our lives.

ANNIE DILLARD

Life can only be understood backwards; but it must be lived forwards.

SØREN KIERKEGAARD

Get Advice from Future You

Imagine that a year from now you've done that big thing you've longed to do—maybe you created a podcast, paid off a loan, or voiced important words to someone in your life. Envision a future you on the far side of a pond, pointing out the stepping-stones you'll cross to get there. Fill in the steps you should be taking, then make plans to start moving toward the destination.

FOLLOW the Cat

The saying originally went: "Curiosity killed the cat, but satisfaction brought it back." That's right, curiosity isn't deadly after all. In fact, it can be quite life-giving. What adventurous paths does your curiosity want you to explore?

Make a plan to follow your curiosity down one new path this week. Go on! It won't kill you.

curiosity
keeps leading
us down
new paths.

WALT DISNEY

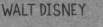

YOU are the average of the five PEOPLE YOU SPEND the MOST time with.

JIM ROHN

FOCUS ON YOUR FLOCK

Happiness is contagious, but so is negativity. Who are the top five people you flock with in real and online life? Write their names below. Circle whether they tend to pull you down or lift you up.

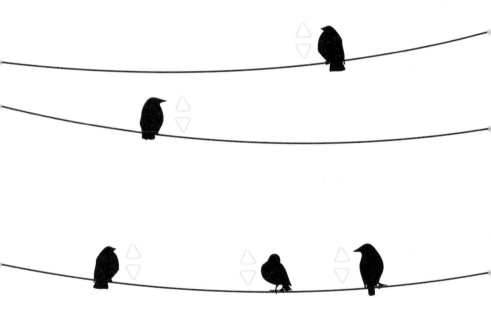

Time to embrace the ones who help you soar and ease back on time spent with the ones who don't.

DON't StOP NOW

Were you on the road to somewhere (a higher-ed degree, launching an Etsy shop) only to find yourself stalled out partway there? Mark the parking spaces where you found a comfort zone but stayed way past the intended time limit.

Time to refuel and get moving again! What steps, tools, and people can help you motor toward your bright goal?

The road
to success
is dotted with
many tempting
parking spaces.

WILL ROGERS

I feel so intensely the delights of shutting oneself up in a little world of one's own...

VIRGINIA WOOLF

HOld, Please!

When the chatter is driving you nuts, it's time to put the world on hold. Turn off your devices. Explain to those certain someones you need some space. Now what would you like to do with your time of sweet serenity? Everything else can wait in these moments.

Leave the Fairy Tale

Holding on to amazing but unrealistic ideas can keep you from discovering all the authentic good in the world. What fairy godmother moment are you waiting for that's holding you back from making your own magic happen?

What clues you into the reality that your carriage is about to turn into a pumpkin?

The more
real you get the
more unreal
the world gets.

JOHN LENNON

Leave your
front and back
door open.
Allow your
thoughts to
come and go.
Just don't
serve them tea.

SHUNRYU SUZUKI

Just Passing Through

Imagine your thoughts as a parade of people passing through your house. You don't want to ignore them, but you don't want them to take up residence either. On the figures below, name a thought you're having, write how it makes you feel as it passes through your house, then wave as it walks out the door, making way for the next thought (name it) and so on.

Sort through the Shatter

If you've thrown your heart and soul into something that fails, it's hard to pick up the pieces and try again. But that's the way to the next better place. Envision your effort as a shattered bowl. What dangerous pieces can you discard, and what promising pieces can you bring to your next endeavor?

Make peace
with your
broken
pieces.

R. H. SIN

It is
our attitude
that
determines
our altitude.

T. D. JAKES

prepare for Takeoff

Think of a challenge you are facing that seems daunting. On the runway below, write all the negative thoughts on the baggage pile that is blocking your plane from taxiing forward, then write the positive thoughts in the jet stream behind the second soaring plane that will propel you upward.

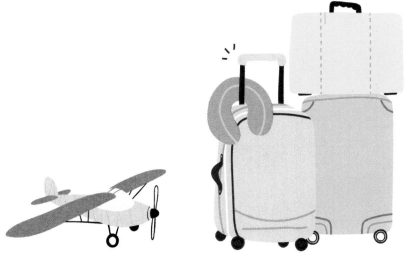

Overstuffed With Stuff?

Ever feel like you spend a ridiculous amount of time fixing, dusting, and maintaining the things that were supposed to make your life easier? Time to lighten the load. Open a drawer or a closet or the garage door, and take a hard look. What items could you sort into the boxes below?

SELL

TRASH

DONATE

The things you own end up owning you.

It's only after you lose everything that you're free to do anything.

CHUCK PALAHNIUK

If you don't prioritize your life, someone else will.

GREG MCKEOWN

GO for the GOld

If you're clear on what matters most to you, you can say no to the unnecessary things that keep steering you off course. List your top ten essentials in life.

1.

2.

3.

4.

5.

6.

7.

8.

9.

10.

Now cross off the seven that aren't as important as your top three. On the medal podiums below, award spots to your top three priorities and focus each day on those prizes.

Scroll or Stroll?

It's easy to spend time wandering through social media, but not all paths are equal. Which social media accounts and connections make you feel like you're headed to a great destination?

Which accounts and connections feel like the darkest part of the forest?

What red flags tell you that it's time to walk away from the screen completely?

There is no Wi-Fi in the forest, but I promise you will find a better connection.

UNKNOWN

These minds
of ours are
magical creation
machines.

MARIE FORLEO

Work Your Magic

Electricity, your favorite songs, and indoor plumbing are only a few of the things that have popped out of someone's imagination and into our reality. If you could release any obstacles (real or perceived), what wild creation would you invent? Describe it or draw it here.

Put Yourself in Place

Where is your happy place? Draw it in the space below surrounded by words that capture the way you feel when you spend time there.

How can you spark these feelings even when you're not in this physical space? Display a photo in a special place? Carry a souvenir? Invoke a scent?

Every human being is born with the capacity for joy, and like the pilot light in your stove, it still burns within you even if you haven't switched on the burners in a while.

INGRID FETELL LEE

It's OK
to live a life
Others don't
understand.

UNKNOWN

Make Your Own Map

Your next step is yours alone—no matter what seems like it's already been mapped out for you. What path do others expect you to follow?

What path would you rather forge for yourself?

What's the first step or two you could take to launch out in that new direction?

Own Your Pleasure

Go ahead, release the pressures as you indulge in your pleasures. What three little things make you secretly smile?

What were the last three experiences that made you laugh out loud?

What makes your day whenever it happens?

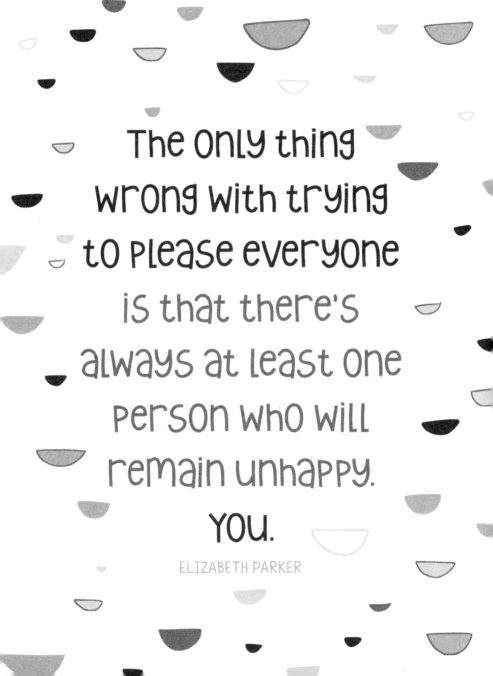

The only thing wrong with trying to please everyone is that there's always at least one person who will remain unhappy. YOU.

ELIZABETH PARKER

Appreciate the NOW

Life is what happens while you're busy making other plans, so release that hefty goal planner for a minute and look at the life around you.

What do you like about where you are right now?

Who are the people that mean the most to you?

What do you love best about the journey you're on?